The heroes of Dart Sports

The greatest players of all time from Peter Wright to Phil Taylor

Foreword

Darts, a sport that demands both precision and strategic skill, has produced numerous outstanding players over the years. These athletes have captured attention not only through their impressive performances but also through their unique personalities and career paths that have shaped the sport. "The Heroes of Dart Sports: The greatest players of all time" is dedicated to these extraordinary talents, offering an in-depth look at their achievements and challenges. The book begins with a detailed examination of Phil Taylor, one of the greatest dart players of all time, and continues with other legends such as Raymond van Barneveld and Michael van Gerwen. Each chapter profiles a player, starting with their beginnings, significant tournament victories, and the moments that turned them into icons of the sport. In addition to the players' biographies, the book also includes analyses of their playing styles, significant matches, and the evolution of their careers. This comprehensive work provides both dart enthusiasts and newcomers to the sport with a valuable resource to fully grasp the fascination and dynamism of darts.

PHIL TAYLOR

Phil Douglas Taylor hit multiple 9-darters on television, a feat he was the first player to achieve multiple times in front of live cameras. Born on August 13, 1960, in Stoke-on-Trent, the darts player is regarded as the most successful in the history of the sport, with a total of sixteen world championship titles. Known by the nickname "The Power," Taylor began his career in the local pubs of his hometown, where he was discovered and financially supported by darts legend Eric Bristow to train professionally and compete in tournaments.

His rise began with winning the Canadian Open in 1990, which earned him a spot in that year's World Darts Championship. There, he surprisingly defeated his mentor Bristow in the final. Taylor dominated the sport throughout the 1990s and 2000s, winning numerous titles and setting new standards, including an impressive average of 107 points per visit in the 2001 World Championship final. He was also instrumental in the founding of the Professional Darts Corporation (PDC) after leaving the British Darts Organisation.

However, his career was not without controversy, including a charge of sexual harassment, which he settled with a fine, leading to a temporary withdrawal of sponsors. Taylor announced his retirement in 2018, ending his professional career with a final appearance at the PDC World Darts Championship, where he lost in the final to Rob Cross.

In the image: Phil Taylor in 2012 at the German Darts Championship at the Tempodrom in Berlin

RAYMOND VAN BARNEVELD

Raymond van Barneveld defeated Phil Taylor, one of the biggest names in darts, in the 2007 PDC World Championship final with a score of 7–6, hitting the maximum score of 180 a remarkable 21 times – a record that stood for many years. The Dutch darts player, born on April 20, 1967, in The Hague, is considered the most successful player from his country and has won a total of five world championship titles, four with the British Darts Organisation (BDO) and one with the Professional Darts Corporation (PDC). Known by the nickname "Barney," van Barneveld began his career while still working as a postal worker.

His switch to the PDC in 2006 marked a turning point in his career. Here, he defeated Taylor multiple times and won major tournaments such as the UK Open. Van Barneveld was also the first darts player to achieve a nine-dart finish live on German television. He repeated this feat several times, including at the 2009 PDC World Championship. However, his career was not without controversy, such as the incident at the 2013 PDC World Championship when his son disrupted an opponent during a match.

After a brief hiatus and an initial retirement in 2020, van Barneveld announced his comeback and shortly thereafter won a ranking tournament. Despite health issues that affected him in some tournaments, he continued to qualify for major events and demonstrated his enduring competitiveness at the highest level.

In the image: Raymond van Barneveld in 2019 at the Unibet Premier League of the PDC

MICHAEL VAN GERWEN

At just 24 years old, Michael van Gerwen won the PDC World Championship in 2014, becoming the youngest player ever to do so. Between January 2014 and January 2021, he dominated as the number one in the PDC Order of Merit, securing additional World Championship titles in 2017 and 2019. With 81 PDC Pro Tour event wins, he surpassed the legend Phil Taylor, who previously held the record with 70 victories. Van Gerwen began his career in the British Darts Organisation (BDO), where he won the World Masters in 2006 and, at just 17 years old, threw a televised nine-darter—a record that wasn't broken until 2024. In 2007, he switched to the PDC and quickly established himself as one of the leading players. Beyond his impressive career, van Gerwen is also successful in his personal life: in 2014, he married his longtime girlfriend Daphne Govers, with whom he has a daughter and a son. His nickname "Mighty Mike" and his walk-on music "Seven Nation Army" by the White Stripes highlight his energetic presence in the world of darts. For his achievements, he was honored with the Order of Orange-Nassau in 2018.

In the picture: Michael van Gerwen 2018 at the European Darts Trophy in Göttingen

Leyland Paints

ERIC BRISTOW

Eric Bristow died in 2018 of a heart attack during a darts event. His impact on the sport is honored through the Eric Bristow Trophy, awarded since 2018 to the winner of the Grand Slam of Darts. Bristow, known as "The Crafty Cockney," significantly shaped the game of darts in the 1980s. He dominated the World Darts Federation rankings for over five years and secured five world championship titles. His career included a total of 82 titles, including 22 WDF and BDO major titles. Bristow played a key role in popularizing darts as a spectator sport.

In 1993, he, along with 15 other top players, initiated the founding of the Professional Darts Corporation (PDC) after breaking away from the British Darts Organisation (BDO). After retiring from professional sports in 2007, Bristow worked as a commentator and expert for Sky Sports.

Bristow was born in London in 1957 and grew up in a working-class family. He attended Hackney Downs Grammar School and was later in a relationship with darts player Maureen Flowers. In 1989, he married Jane Higginbotham, with whom he had two children before they divorced in 2005.

His participation in the reality show "I'm a Celebrity...Get Me Out of Here!" in 2012, where he finished in fourth place, showcased his versatile personality. Despite his successes, Bristow also faced challenges, such as the mental condition dartitis, which prevented him from throwing darts properly and impacted his career.

In the image: Eric Bristow in 2015 at a charity match before the Betway Premier League Darts in Liverpool

viaplay

JOHN LOWE

On October 13, 1984, John Lowe made history by achieving the first televised nine-dart finish against Keith Deller, earning a prize of £100,000. Known as "Old Stoneface," Lowe established himself as one of England's leading dart players, particularly during the 1970s and 1980s. One of his most remarkable achievements is winning the World Championship in three different decades: 1979, 1987, and 1993, making him, alongside Phil Taylor, one of the few players to accomplish this feat. In 1993, he was also involved in founding the World Darts Council, now known as the Professional Darts Corporation.

Lowe also succeeded in major tournaments, including two victories at the BDO World Masters (1976 and 1980) and a win at the News of the World Darts Championship in 1981. In his later career with the PDC, he did not secure any major titles but achieved respectable results in the 1990s and early 2000s, including semifinal appearances at the World Championship and the World Matchplay. In 2005, he retired from professional darts after a 30-year career.

Lowe participated in 28 consecutive World Championships before losing his final match in 2005. He continued attempting to qualify for further World Championships until 2008 but was unsuccessful. In 2022, he took part in the inaugural World Seniors Darts Championship but announced after a loss that it would likely be his last appearance in the tournament. John Lowe is married to his wife Karen and has published two books about darts.

In the image: John Lowe 1995 at the Pro Darts WDC

John Lowe
unicorn
proton cars

GARY ANDERSON

Anderson's skills on stage became particularly evident when he won the PDC World Championship back-to-back in 2015 and 2016, defeating 16-time world champion Phil Taylor in the 2015 final. Gary Anderson, born on December 22, 1970, in Musselburgh, Scotland, is an outstanding darts player, best known for his achievements in the Professional Darts Corporation (PDC). Anderson, also known as "The Flying Scotsman," began his career in the British Darts Organisation (BDO), where he quickly made a name for himself. His walk-on music, "Jump Around" by House of Pain, reflects his energetic style.

Anderson's career took a significant turn when he switched to the PDC in 2009. This move followed impressive performances in the BDO, including winning the Topic International Darts League and the Bullit World Darts Trophy in 2007. In the PDC, he quickly found success, including a runner-up finish at the 2011 World Championship and winning the Premier League Darts in 2011.

Anderson's achievements are marked by high averages and spectacular finishes, including several nine-dart finishes, the highest accolade in darts.

Despite some health setbacks and fluctuating performances in subsequent years, Anderson remained a central figure in the sport. He won the 2018 World Matchplay and the Champions League of Darts and continued to achieve high placements in major tournaments.

In addition to his sporting success, Anderson has also built a family and is the father of four children.

In the image: Gary Anderson in 2019 at the German Darts Masters in the Lanxess Arena, Cologne

RIX
unicorn

DENNIS PRIESTLEY

Dennis Priestley won the 1991 BDO World Championship and the inaugural PDC World Darts Championship in 1994, making him one of the standout players of his era. Between 1996 and 2000, he reached the PDC World Darts Championship final four more times but was defeated on each occasion by Phil Taylor. Known as "The Menace," Priestley began his professional darts career at nearly 40 years old and first gained attention in 1989 when he reached the final of the News of the World Darts Championship.

Priestley was also a founding member of the World Darts Council, which split from the British Darts Organisation in 1993. Despite his on-stage successes, he often struggled in televised events and suffered several early exits at the World Championship. His career was overshadowed by health issues, including a prostate cancer diagnosis in 2007, which temporarily sidelined him from the sport. Nevertheless, he made a successful comeback in 2008, reaching the semifinals of the US Open.

Priestley appeared in the 2007 Premier League Darts, securing a spot in the semifinals. In 2009, he won the US Open after failing to qualify for the Grand Slam of Darts. However, his performances declined, and in 2011, he lost his place in the top 32 of the PDC Order of Merit. In 2012, he reached the final of Players Championship Event 17 but was defeated by Simon Whitlock. Priestley retired from professional darts in early 2015 but remained active in exhibition events.

In the image: Dennis Priestley in 2012 during the Ladbrokes World Darts Championships at Alexandra Palace, London

WINMAU
dennispriestley.com

JAMES WADE

James Martin Wade is the most successful darts player never to have won a World Championship title. Despite reaching the finals of major tournaments multiple times, including the World Matchplay and the PDC World Darts Championship, this triumph eluded him. With eleven victories in televised tournaments, he ranks behind only legends like Phil Taylor and Michael van Gerwen in the Professional Darts Corporation (PDC). Known as "The Machine" due to his remarkable consistency, especially in hitting doubles, Wade has established himself as the most successful left-handed player in darts history. Born on April 6, 1983, in Aldershot, Hampshire, he began his professional career in 2001 in the World Darts Federation before switching to the PDC in 2004. His first major success came with his victory at the World Matchplay in 2007, followed by other significant titles such as the World Grand Prix in the same year and the UK Open in 2008. In 2009, he claimed the Darts Premier League and repeated his success at the World Grand Prix in 2010. His career is also notable for achieving nine-dart finishes, including historic moments like two nine-darters in a single televised match in 2014. Beyond his sporting achievements, Wade is also known for his openness about his bipolar disorder and serves as an ambassador for the charity "bipolar UK." On a personal note, he has been married to Samantha Marsh since 2015, and the couple has two sons.

In the image: James Wade in 2016 at the European Darts Matchplay in the Inselparkhalle, Hamburg

PETER WRIGHT

Peter Wright holds the record for the highest ever live-recorded average of 123.5 points. The Scottish darts player, born on March 10, 1970, in Livingston, won the PDC World Championship in 2020 and 2022 and reached the number one spot in the PDC Order of Merit between March and July 2022, as well as briefly in October 2022. Wright is the first Scot to achieve this position.

His darts career began at the age of 13 when he received his first set of darts as a gift. Despite financial difficulties that prevented him from buying his own dartboard, Wright practiced on painted targets on trees. By the age of 17, he was already one of the best local darts players in London. His professional career started in 1995 at the BDO World Championship, though he was eliminated early. It wasn't until 2004 that Wright joined the PDC and reached the final of the Eastbourne Open.

Wright's breakthrough in the PDC came years later, after working with a hypnotist to address his nervousness. In 2009, he debuted at the Las Vegas Desert Classics and qualified for the World Matchplay. In 2012, he won his first PDC title in Ireland and reached the quarterfinals of the Players Championship Finals.

In 2014, Wright surprisingly secured second place at the PDC World Darts Championship and received a wildcard for the Premier League Darts. These achievements allowed him to overcome his financial struggles and continue his career. In 2017, he won his first major title at the UK Open and followed it up with further victories.

Wright, known for his brightly colored hair and vibrant performances, remains a key figure in professional darts despite occasional dips in form and health challenges.

In the image: Peter Wright in 2014 at the World Cup of Darts in Hamburg

DESIRA
COPYFAX
bwin
RedDragon
LoudMouth

ROB CROSS

Rob Cross sensationally won the PDC World Championship in 2018 during his debut and climbed to 3rd place in the world rankings. This triumph earned him an invitation to the 2018 Premier League Darts. Born on September 21, 1990, in Pembury, Cross was originally an electrician and received the nickname "Voltage" due to his former profession. He is the father of four children.

His professional darts career began in 2016 when he earned a Tour Card by participating in the PDC Challenge Tour. 2017 marked the start of his professional journey, during which he won his first tournament on the PDC Pro Tour. Cross qualified for the World Matchplay and reached the round of 16.

In 2019, Cross won the World Matchplay and the European Darts Championship, solidifying his status as one of the leading players. Despite some challenges in the following years, including an early exit at the 2020 World Championship, Cross showed a resurgence in form in 2021 and once again won the European Darts Championship.

In 2022 and 2023, Cross was unable to replicate his earlier successes but did reach the final of the Grand Slam of Darts in 2023.

In the image: Rob Cross in 2017 at the PDC Darts Grand Prix in Sindelfingen, Germany

JOCKY WILSON

Jocky Wilson, known for his high alcohol consumption during games and for losing all his teeth early, which he attributed to poisoned water, won the BDO World Championships in 1982 and 1989. The Scottish darts player, who became a two-time world champion, had a remarkable career that spanned from 1979 to 1995. Wilson was born on March 22, 1950, in Kirkcaldy and passed away there on March 24, 2012. His childhood was challenging; after his parents were deemed unfit, he grew up in an orphanage. His darts career began in a local pub, where the landlady gifted him a used dartboard.

Wilson served in the British Army from 1966 to 1968 and later worked in various jobs before honing his darting skills during a period of unemployment. His breakthrough came in 1979 when he won a tournament and decided to turn professional. In 1993, he participated in the founding of the Professional Darts Corporation (PDC) but was unable to replicate his earlier successes there. His last significant appearance was at the 1995 World Matchplay.

After withdrawing from public life, Wilson lived reclusively and declined interviews. He suffered from severe illnesses linked to his lifestyle and passed away in 2012. His life and career were featured in a documentary.

In the image: Jocky Wilson 1989 playing darts

BOB ANDERSON

At the age of just seven, Bob Anderson threw his first "180," an impressive start to a darts career that would see him crowned World Champion in 1988. Anderson, known as "The Limestone Cowboy," won the World Professional Darts Championship that year and claimed the World Masters Championship three years in a row between 1986 and 1988. Originally, he was also a talented javelin thrower and was nominated for the 1968 Olympic Games but had to withdraw due to a broken arm.

His darts career was marked by numerous successes, including victories in major tournaments such as the British Gold Cup and the MFI World Matchplay. Despite undergoing back surgery in 1990, which threatened his career, he made a successful comeback and won additional titles. Anderson also contributed to the sport off the field by founding the Bob Anderson Classic, a significant tournament held from 2002 to 2005, and developing the training program "Bob's 27."

In the later years of his career, he joined the Professional Darts Corporation (PDC) and reached the semifinals of World Championships there as well. Even after retiring from professional play in 2008, Anderson remained connected to the sport through participation in exhibitions and senior tournaments.

In the picture: Bob Anderson 2017 at the Cologne Darts Gala in the Lanxess Arena, Cologne

McDart.de
unicorn

KEITH DELLER

Keith Kelvin Deller became the first qualifier to win the Embassy World Professional Darts Championship in 1983, defeating the favored Eric Bristow 6-5 in the final. The decisive leg was particularly legendary, as Deller secured victory with a spectacular 138-point finish – a throw now famously known as the "Keith-Deller-Finish." With this win, he became the youngest world champion in darts history at the time. Despite this early success, Deller was unable to defend his title the following year and exited the tournament early.

In 1993, Deller was one of the co-founders of the World Darts Council, later renamed the Professional Darts Corporation. His career reached another peak in 1998 with a semifinal appearance at the World Championship and the World Matchplay. Despite further participation in major tournaments, additional significant successes eluded him.

Beyond his playing career, Deller also worked as the manager of two-time world champion Adrian Lewis and served as a spotter for Sky Sports, occasionally collaborating with his former World Championship opponent Bristow. In 2022 and 2023, he participated in the Seniors World Championship but was unable to achieve notable victories.

In the image: Keith Deller 1995 at the Pro Darts WDC

RILEY
proto bars

ROD HARRINGTON

Rodney "Rod" Harrington was ranked number 1 in the PDC world rankings from 1995 to 1996 and again from 1998 to 2000. One of his greatest achievements came in 1991 when he won the Winmau World Masters, defeating Phil Taylor in the final—a rare moment where Taylor lost in a major tournament final. In 1998, Harrington won the World Matchplay against Ronnie Baxter and successfully defended his title the following year against Peter Manley. Until 2007, he was, alongside Taylor, the only player to defend a PDC major title.

Harrington, also known as The Prince of Style, reached the finals of several major PDC tournaments. In 1995, he made it to the final of the PDC World Championship but lost to Taylor. He began his career in the BDO before transitioning to the PDC. After his active playing career, Harrington remained involved in darts as a PDC director and as an expert and commentator for SkySports. He also worked as a manager for other players, such as Colin Lloyd. On September 5, 2022, Harrington retired from his roles at the PDC. His career includes numerous other titles, including multiple victories at the Golden Harvest North American Cup and various European Open tournaments.

In the image: Rod Harrington 1995 at the Pro Darts WDC

DURRO

RONNIE BAXTER

Ronnie Baxter reached the final of the Embassy World Professional Darts Championship twice in a row in 1999 and 2000 but was defeated on both occasions. Known as "The Rocket" and famous for his robotic throwing style, he made a name for himself in the darts world. Initially active in the North American darts scene during the 1980s, he later gained recognition in England as well. In the 1990s, Baxter was among the leading darts players worldwide. Despite these losses and other runner-up finishes in major tournaments, he achieved the number one spot in the WDF rankings, thanks in part to victories at the British Matchplay in 1992 and 1998.

In 2002, Baxter switched to the Professional Darts Corporation (PDC), where he quickly became one of the top players, even though he never won a major tournament. In the early 2000s, he secured several tournament wins and achieved high placements in key competitions, including the quarterfinals of the World Championship and the semifinals of the World Grand Prix. Despite a decline in success in later years, Baxter remained competitive on the Pro Tour until 2013.

His career began to wind down when he failed to qualify for the World Championship in 2016 for the first time since 1991. In 2018, he retired from active competition in the PDC after playing one final tournament. Since 2022, Baxter has occasionally participated in events on the World Seniors Darts Tour, though without notable success so far. On a personal note, Baxter has experienced some life changes, including separating from his wife and moving back to Blackpool, where he had previously run a guesthouse.

In the image: Ronnie Baxter in 2011 at the PDC World Matchplay in the Winter Gardens, Blackpool

sky BET mobile
TOMMY'S DARTS
WKD

TERRY JENKINS

Terry Jenkins hit his first nine-dart finish at a World Championship in 2014. Despite regularly reaching the finals of major PDC tournaments, he never managed to win a title. His best performance at a World Championship came in 2011 when he reached the semifinals. His most successful year was 2007, when he finished runner-up in the Holsten Premier League, the World Matchplay, and the Las Vegas Desert Classic. Additionally, he won two PDPA Players Championships, which earned him fourth place in the world rankings.

Jenkins, born on September 26, 1963, in Ledbury, Herefordshire, started playing darts in 1970 and began his professional career with the British Darts Organisation (BDO), though he never qualified for the World Championship there. In 2003, he switched to the Professional Darts Corporation (PDC). At the end of 2016, he announced he would scale back his career after the 2017 World Championship and subsequently stopped competing on the European Tour. His last World Championship match was in 2017, where he lost in the second round.

In 2022 and 2023, Jenkins participated in the Seniors World Championship, reaching the semifinals in 2022 and exiting in the second round in 2023. Jenkins is married and the father of three children.

In the image: Terry Jenkins in 2011 at the 888.com Premier League Darts in the Metro Radio Arena, Newcastle

The Bull

MERVYN KING

During the first lockdown of the COVID-19 pandemic, Mervyn King worked as a delivery driver for Amazon and founded a construction company in 2021. Alongside his darts career, King is also a motorsport enthusiast and had the opportunity to become a racing driver in his youth but chose darts instead. Born on March 15, 1966, in Ipswich, King started playing darts at the age of twelve and joined the local darts league at fourteen. His father played a crucial role in his early development by giving him a dartboard and insisting he practice under competitive conditions. The death of his father in 2010 had a profound impact on King's form and performance.

King began his professional career in the British Darts Organisation (BDO), where he played from 1995 to 2007 before switching to the Professional Darts Corporation (PDC). During his time in the BDO, he reached several major finals and won the 2004 World Masters. In the PDC, he has reached seven major finals so far but has not won a title. King is known for his friendship with darts player Peter Wright, with whom he frequently trains. He lives near Wright in Bradwell on Sea, Norfolk.

In the image: Mervyn King in 2019 at the European Darts Open in the Ostermann-Arena, Leverkusen

WINMAU
DUCATI
Norwich
LES BURONS

CHRIS MASON

Chris Mason, an English darts player, was sentenced to a three-year prison term in 2003, of which he served about one year. Despite his personal challenges, he achieved significant success in both the British Darts Organisation (BDO) and the Professional Darts Corporation (PDC). He began his career with a victory at the Scottish Open in 1995. Mason reached the semifinals of the BDO World Professional Darts Championship twice, in 1999 and 2000, showcasing remarkable comebacks, including one against then-world champion Raymond van Barneveld. He also made it to the semifinals of the Winmau World Masters in 2000 and the World Matchplay in 1998.

His time in the PDC from 2000 to 2014 was also marked by success, including a nine-darter against Sean Palfrey at the Players Championships in 2004. However, health issues forced him to reconsider his active career, leading to surgery in 2008 for a nerve problem in his elbow. Following this, Mason also appeared as a co-presenter for darts broadcasts on ITV4.

He is married and a father of three children. In 2023, he returned to the Seniors World Championship, where he was eliminated in the first match against Terry Jenkins.

In the image: Chris Mason 2023 during the World Senior Darts Championship at the Circus Tavern, Purfleet, United Kingdom

RBS
WSDT
Metal Detecting

WAYNE MARDLE

Wayne Mardle was the first player to defeat Phil Taylor in the quarterfinals of the 2008 World Darts Championship before being eliminated in the semifinals. Despite his popularity and reaching 5th place in the world rankings, Mardle never managed to win a major PDC tournament. His best results were reaching the finals of the Las Vegas Desert Classic in 2004 and 2005, where he lost to Phil Taylor on both occasions, as well as the semifinals of the 2006 PDC World Championship.

Mardle, nicknamed "Hawaii 501," started playing darts at the age of 11 and hit his first 180, the highest possible score with three darts, just two weeks after he began playing. He owes his nickname to the Hawaiian shirts he has worn during appearances since 1998, as well as a nod to the starting score of a leg in darts and the TV series Hawaii Five-O.

Mardle, who has been married to his wife Donna since 2002, ended his competitive career in 2012 and has since worked as an expert for Sky Sports at major darts tournaments. He also appeared at the Celebrity Darts World Cup in 2017.

In the image: Wayne Mardle at the Gude 3 Darts Open in the Ballsporthalle, Frankfurt, 2023

TICKET
501
SCORE
LEGS
SETS
Hawaii
501

ANDY HAMILTON

Andrew Hamilton's greatest achievement was reaching the final of the 2012 PDC World Darts Championship, where he lost to Adrian Lewis. Known as "The Hammer," the darts player from Stoke-on-Trent established himself in the darts world despite this defeat, reaching several semi-finals and finals at PDC major tournaments, though he was unable to win any. He began his career at the age of 16 but had to take a 20-year break before making his television debut at the 2004 UK Open. Hamilton's performances earned him a spot in the 2012 Premier League Darts. After losing his PDC Tour Card in 2018, he switched to the BDO, where he qualified for the 2019 World Championship but exited early. He returned to the PDC and won a Challenge Tour event in 2022. Despite multiple attempts at Q-School, he was unable to regain his Tour Card. Hamilton's training partners included multiple world champion Phil Taylor and later Colin Osborne. Despite fluctuating success on the PDC Challenge Tour and the World Seniors Darts Tour, Hamilton remains a well-known figure in the world of darts.

In the image: Andy Hamilton 2024 during the JenningsBet Champion of Champions Tour at Viva, Blackpool

GSbet

STEVE BEATON

Steve Beaton holds the record for the most consecutive World Championship appearances in darts history – an incredible 33 times, including 10 with the BDO and 23 with the PDC. The "Bronzed Adonis," as he is known, won the BDO World Championship in 1996, defeating Richie Burnett in the final, earning him a prize of £36,000. Beaton began his professional darts career in 1984 and achieved his first major success in 1993 by winning the World Masters. After further successes, including multiple team titles at the WDF Europe Cups, he switched to the PDC in 2001, where he initially found some success, such as winning the Vauxhall Spring Open in 2001. However, major victories eluded him, and Beaton struggled to regain his earlier form. Nevertheless, he achieved occasional successes on the Pro Tour, including winning the Players Championship in 2009 and 2017, as well as the German Darts Masters in 2013 on the European Darts Tour. Beaton, who also works as a driving instructor and lives with his wife Nanette in Earl Shilton, has announced that he will retire after the 2025 World Championship.

In the image: Steve Beaton at the European Darts Grand Prix in Sindelfingen, 2015

APL
TheWigleyGroup

ANDY FORDHAM

On July 15, 2021, Andy Fordham passed away at the age of 59 due to severe organ failure. His death caused great sorrow in the darts world, and many colleagues, including world champions Adrian Lewis and Rob Cross, expressed their condolences. Fordham, known as "The Viking," was an outstanding English darts player who won the BDO World Championship title in 2004 by defeating Mervyn King in the final. Despite this triumph, he struggled with health issues exacerbated by his significant overweight and high alcohol consumption. These led to a collapse in 2007, after which he took a break to focus on his health.

Fordham later returned to darts but was unable to replicate his earlier successes. He participated in various tournaments, including the PDC Pro Tour, and reached several last-16 rounds. His last major final was in 2017 at the Isle of Man Open. Born on February 2, 1962, in Bristol, he spent his childhood in Charlton, London, attending Charlton Manor Primary School and Eaglesfield Secondary School. Professionally, Fordham initially worked as a customs officer and later ran a darts pub in Dartford with his wife Jenny, whom he met in the early 1980s and married in 2000. The couple had two children, Ray and Emily.

In the image: Bobby George, Johnny Vegas, and Andy Fordham, known as The Viking, at Maxim Darts

Andy
THE
VIKING
Fordham

DARYL GURNEY

Daryl Gurney hit a nine-darter in 2023 at the Players Championship, one of the rarest and most impressive achievements in darts. In 2018, he claimed his second major title at the Players Championship Finals by defeating Michael van Gerwen in the final. His career reached further heights with his victory at the German Darts Championship in 2019 and a top-3 ranking in the world standings. Gurney continued his rise by reaching the quarterfinals of the PDC World Championship in 2017 and winning the World Grand Prix. He quickly made a name for himself in the PDC by qualifying for the 2013 World Championship and securing notable victories, including one against van Gerwen. His consistent performances led to multiple semifinal appearances and eventually his first PDC major semifinal at the Players Championship Finals in 2015.

He began his darts career in 2004 with the British Darts Organisation (BDO), achieving his first major breakthrough in 2009 by reaching the final of the WDF Europe Cup and advancing to the last 16 of the BDO World Championship. After several tournament wins in 2012, including the England Masters and the Northern Ireland Open, he transitioned to the Professional Darts Corporation (PDC) in 2013.

In the image: Daryl Gurney at the Cologne Darts Gala in the Lanxess Arena, Cologne, 2017

WINMAU
TOTAL
HIRE & SALES

GERWYN PRICE

In 2021, Gerwyn Price became the first Welshman to win the PDC World Darts Championship, reaching the top of the PDC world rankings. Price, known by the nickname "The Iceman," had already celebrated his first major success in 2018 by winning the Grand Slam of Darts. Prior to that, he had won the World Grand Prix and the World Series of Darts Finals in 2020. However, his sporting career initially began in rugby, where he played as a hooker in the Welsh Premier Division and for the Glasgow Warriors. A hand injury in 2014 forced him to end his rugby career, after which he fully dedicated himself to darts, a sport he had been pursuing in parallel since 2010.

Price is also known for his controversial moments, including loud celebrations and confrontations with other players, which have earned him a bit of a bad-boy image in the darts scene. Despite initial losses after earning his Tour Card at the PDC Qualifying School in 2014, he quickly made progress and reached the final of the UK Open in 2017.

In the image: Gerwyn Price at the FlyDSA Arena, Sheffield, 2019

VALLEY
WATER SERVICES LTD
JASIC
The power in inverter technology

MICHAEL SMITH

In 2023, Michael Smith reached a career high when he defeated Michael van Gerwen in the World Championship final, throwing a nine-darter in the process. This triumph brought him to the top of the PDC Order of Merit for the first time and crowned him as the Professional Darts Corporation (PDC) World Champion, after previously finishing as runner-up twice. Despite an early exit at the 2024 World Championship, Smith remains a key figure in the sport of darts. On December 1, 2023, he was awarded honorary citizenship of his hometown, St Helens.

Smith's career in professional darts began notably in 2010 when he reached the last 32 at the UK Open. His first major success came in 2011 when he won the UK Open Qualifier 2. Since then, he has been a regular on the PDC circuit. Despite early exits in World Championships, Smith quickly established himself and won the 2013 PDC World Youth Championship.

His breakthrough on the world stage came in 2014 when he defeated darts legend Phil Taylor at the World Championship, although he was later eliminated from the tournament. Smith's rise continued, and in 2016, he qualified for the Premier League Darts for the first time. In the following years, he reached several major finals, including the World Championship in 2019 and 2022, but it wasn't until 2022 at the Grand Slam of Darts that he secured his first major title.

He is known by the nickname "Bully Boy."

In the image: Michael Smith Bully Boy at the Celebrity Darts World Cup at the Maritim Hotel, Düsseldorf, 2023

schauinsland reisen
Andyfreight
unicorn

IAN WHITE

Ian White hit several nine-darters, including one against Mensur Suljović in 2019. Born on August 17, 1970, in Stoke-on-Trent, the English darts player began his career in the British Darts Organisation (BDO) and first gained attention in 1997 when he reached the final of the News of the World Darts Championship but lost to Phil Taylor. After a break, he returned in 2005 and regularly competed in BDO tournaments. In 2009, he claimed his first major titles at the Antwerp Open and the Denmark Open.

In 2010, White switched to the Professional Darts Corporation (PDC) and soon reached his first PDC Pro Tour final. However, despite several final appearances, he was unable to secure a PDC major title. His best performance at a World Championship came in 2014 when he reached the quarterfinals.

Since 2020, White's success has declined, with early exits in major tournaments and a drop in the world rankings. Nevertheless, he managed to win a Players Championship in 2020 and reached the last 16 at the European Darts Championship. His World Championship results vary, with his best performance being a last-16 finish in 2017. White has won multiple Pro Tour titles and performed well at the Players Championship Finals but has never reached the final of a major tournament.

In the image: Ian White at the PDC World Darts Championship at Alexandra Palace, London, 2023

PADDYPOWER
unicorn

SIMON WHITLOCK

Whitlock is also known for his unusually rough dart points, which have sparked discussions about a possible ban due to their excessive damage to dartboards. In 2022, he won his second major title alongside Damon Heta at the World Cup. In 2018, Whitlock reached the final of the European Darts Championship and the semifinals of the World Cup of Darts. He remained a prominent figure in the darts world, reaching the last 16 of the PDC World Darts Championship in 2019.

Despite a temporary career slump that saw him drop out of the top 16, Whitlock regained his form in 2016, winning two Players Championship events. He also reached the quarterfinals of the World Grand Prix and the World Cup of Darts. In 2017, he continued to make an impact by winning two UK Open Qualifiers and advancing to the semifinals of the German Darts Masters.

Whitlock also achieved notable success at the European Darts Championship, winning his first major title in 2012. He continued his streak of success by reaching the semifinals of the PDC World Darts Championship in 2012. In 2013, he once again qualified for the Premier League and reached the final of the European Darts Championship.

In the PDC, Whitlock reached the final of the World Championship in 2010, finishing as runner-up. This achievement earned him £100,000 in prize money and solidified his position in the darts world. He also qualified for the 2010 Premier League Darts, where he finished in second place. On the PDC Pro Tour, he reached multiple finals, winning six of them. He also delivered strong performances in major tournaments, including a semifinal appearance at the 2010 UK Open and the World Matchplay.

Simon Whitlock, known as "The Wizard," is an Australian darts player active in the Professional Darts Corporation (PDC). His nickname and unconventional finishing style are reflected in his walk-on music, "Down Under" by Men at Work. Whitlock began his career in 2002, quickly winning the Australian Masters. After switching to the British Darts Organisation (BDO) in 2003, he returned to the PDC in 2009 and experienced a meteoric rise.

In the image: Simon Whitlock at the William Hill World Darts Championship at Alexandra Palace, London, 2018

Leyland

STEPHEN BUNTING

Stephen Bunting won the British Darts Organisation (BDO) World Championship title in January 2014 by defeating Alan Norris 7-4 in the final. Shortly after this triumph, he switched to the Professional Darts Corporation (PDC). Bunting, born on April 9, 1985, in Liverpool and known by the nickname "The Bullet" due to the high speed of his throws, first gained attention as a teenager when he won the Lancashire Open final in 2000. In the following years, he established himself as one of the greatest young talents in darts, winning several youth tournaments, including the British Teenage Open and the WDF World Youth Cup in 2001. He claimed his first major title in the men's category in 2012 at the World Masters.

After his move to the PDC in 2014, Bunting quickly found his footing and qualified for major tournaments. His greatest success in the PDC came with his victory at the Masters in 2024. Bunting has solidified his place on the PDC Tour through his performances and has reached the final stages of major tournaments multiple times. His career has been marked by highs and lows, including several quarterfinal appearances at the PDC World Darts Championship and a semifinal in 2021. Bunting remains a prominent figure in professional darts, known for his fast and precise throws.

In the image: Stephen Bunting at the World Professional Darts Championship in Lakeside, 2011

JOHN SMITH'S
jackpotjoy.com

MENSUR SULJOVIĆ

Mensur Suljović won the Champions League of Darts in 2017, marking his greatest achievement to date. The Serbian darts player, who competes for Austria, also achieved notable success in the PDC, including reaching the Last 16 of the 2011 World Championship, where he became the first German-speaking player to advance to this stage. In 2016, he claimed his first PDC tournament victory at the International Darts Open. Despite some losses in key matches, such as the 2016 European Darts Championship final against Michael van Gerwen, Suljović has solidified his presence in the darts world.

Known as "The Gentle," Suljović began his career in Vienna, initially excelling in soft-tip darts, where he won multiple European and World Championships. He later transitioned to steel-tip darts and reached the Last 16 of the Winmau World Masters in 2000. Despite a two-year break due to dartitis, he resumed his career and joined the Professional Darts Corporation (PDC) in 2007.

In addition to his sporting achievements, Suljović ran a pub in Vienna but later stepped back to fully focus on darts. He has lived in Vienna with his family since 1993 and, despite his long career and dedication to Austria, does not hold Austrian citizenship.

In the image: Mensur Suljovic during his match against Ryan Searle at the William Hill World Darts Championship in Alexandra Palace, London, 2018

BULL'S

JOE CULLEN

His greatest achievement was winning the Masters 2022, a major tournament where he defeated Dave Chisnall in the final. Cullen continued his streak of success by winning the European Darts Matchplay in 2019, his biggest title to date, by beating Michael van Gerwen in the final. Despite some setbacks at World Championships, where he often exited early, he remained a consistent presence in the upper ranks of the PDC.

In 2017, he broke into the world's Top 32 and won his first Pro Tour event. Additionally, he reached the semifinals of a major tournament at the European Darts Championship 2018. In 2011, Cullen claimed his first PDC title on the Youth Tour and secured his first World Championship victory at the PDC World Darts Championship 2012, though he was eliminated in the first round.

His career began in 2008 when he joined the PDC directly, without prior experience in the British Darts Organisation. His first significant tournament was the UK Open 2008, where he won his opening match but was eliminated in the second round.

In the image: Joe Cullen at the European Darts Grand Prix in Glaspalast, Sindelfingen, 2023

WINMAU
inter
wetten
TXODDS

JONNY CLAYTON

2021 was an extraordinary year for Jonny Clayton, during which he won four major titles, more than any other player that year. He triumphed at the Masters, secured two Players Championships, and capped off his season with victory in the Premier League Darts, where he claimed the title as a debutant. 2020 had already marked a turning point in his career when he threw his first nine-darter at the UK Open and, alongside Gerwyn Price, won the World Cup of Darts.

Clayton, born on October 4, 1974, in Pontyberem, Wales, is known by the nickname "The Ferret," which he earned for his agility during his time as an amateur rugby player. In 2015, he joined the Professional Darts Corporation (PDC) and secured a Tour Card on the final day of Qualifying School. He made his PDC World Championship debut in 2017, where he defeated Gerwyn Price in the first round but was eliminated in the second round. That same year, he won his first tournament on the PDC Pro Tour and reached the final of the Players Championship Finals, where he lost to Michael van Gerwen.

Clayton continued his success, reaching the quarterfinals of the World Championship in 2022. He also won Players Championship 12 in 2023 and claimed his second victory at the Austrian Darts Open. Despite facing challenges in the second half of the year, including the loss of his father, Clayton remained a key figure in the darts world. He is married, a father of two, and has continued his profession as a plasterer alongside his darts career.

In the image: Jonny Clayton at the Darts World Championship in Frankfurt am Main, 2018

RedDragon
trade

NATHAN ASPINALL

In 2023, Aspinall won the World Matchplay, his second major tournament, and reached the final of the World Series Finals. However, his performances at the World Championship and in the Premier League showed inconsistencies, as he either exited early or narrowly missed the playoffs. In 2019, he won the UK Open and the US Darts Masters, marking his rise in the darts world. At the 2020 PDC World Darts Championship, he once again reached the semifinals. That same year, he competed in the Premier League Darts and made it to the final. The years 2021 and 2022 were marked by highs and lows; he hit two nine-darters but also struggled with an injury that affected his performance. Despite this, he reached the finals of the World Grand Prix and the Grand Slam of Darts in 2022.

In 2018, Aspinall claimed his first victory on the PDC Pro Tour at the Players Championships in Barnsley. This success earned him a spot in his first World Championship, where he achieved remarkable wins, including one against Gerwyn Price, and advanced to the semifinals. Nathan Aspinall, born on July 15, 1991, in Stockport, is an English darts player who competes in the Professional Darts Corporation (PDC) and is known by the nickname "The Asp." He began his career in 2012, attempting to qualify for the PDC Pro Tour through the Development Tour and Q-School. He eventually succeeded in 2015, securing his place on the Pro Tour for the 2016 and 2017 seasons. That same year, he reached the final of the PDC World Youth Championship but narrowly lost to Max Hopp.

In the image: Nathan Aspinall at the European Darts Grand Prix in Sindelfingen, 2019

PRESTIGE
BUILDING SUPPLIES LTD
easy-trim
TARGET

DIMITRI VAN DEN BERGH

Dimitri Van den Bergh recently confirmed his top form by winning the UK Open 2024, another major title that briefly elevated him to 7th place in the world rankings. His career had already peaked in 2020 when, during the COVID-19 pandemic, he trained intensively with world champion Peter Wright and subsequently won the World Matchplay, catapulting him into the top 10 of the world rankings. Despite some setbacks, such as early exits in major tournaments and a COVID-19-related cancellation, Van den Bergh remained a prominent figure in the darts world.

The Belgian, known as "The Dreammaker," began his career in 2012 in the BDO, where he won the British Teen Open before switching to the PDC in 2013. He quickly made progress there, winning several Youth Tour events and making his World Championship debut in 2015, where he surprisingly defeated Ian White. Despite initial struggles in the PDC, including the threat of dropping out of the top 100, Van den Bergh solidified his position through consistent improvements and key victories. In 2017, he won the PDC World Youth Championship and reached the quarterfinals of the 2018 World Championship. He also showcased his skills at the Grand Slam of Darts and the German Darts Masters, delivering impressive performances.

In the image: Dimitri Van den Bergh at the Dart PDC World Cup Team Championship in Hamburg, 2019

BETVICTOR
BETVICTOR
BETVICTOR

GLEN DURRANT

Glen Durrant won the 2020 PDC Premier League Darts as a debutant, securing prize money of £250,000. Prior to this, he had claimed the BDO World Championship three consecutive times (2017-2019), elevating him to the ranks of darting legends like Eric Bristow. His career began in 2005 in the BDO, where he initially remained without major success until 2014, when he achieved his first tournament victories and qualified for the World Championship. From 2015 onwards, Durrant dominated the BDO, winning multiple tournaments, including two major titles at the World Masters and the Zuiderduin Masters.

After switching to the PDC in 2019, he immediately earned a Tour Card and quickly celebrated early successes, including a victory over reigning PDC World Champion Michael van Gerwen at the World Matchplay. Despite a strong start in the PDC, including a semifinal appearance at the 2019 World Grand Prix, Durrant experienced a dip in form starting in 2020. He lost all his matches in the 2021 Premier League and delivered weak performances in other tournaments, which ultimately led to him losing his Tour Card at the end of 2022 and temporarily pausing his professional career. Despite these setbacks, Durrant plans to participate in the 2024 Q-School and competed in the 2023 World Seniors Darts Championship. Since 2023, he has also been working as a TV pundit for Sky Sports.

In the image: Glen Durrant and Dave Chisnall at the BoyleSports World Grand Prix Darts at the Citywest Hotel, Dublin, 2019

ULTIMATE
TARGET

JEFFREY DE ZWAAN

At the 2018 World Matchplay, Jeffrey de Zwaan, ranked 68th in the world, sensationally defeated the number one player, Michael van Gerwen, and reached the semifinals. De Zwaan, born on March 26, 1996, in Rijswijk, began his career in the British Darts Organisation (BDO), where he won the World Youth Masters in 2012. A year later, he participated in the Zuiderduin Masters but was eliminated in the group stage.

In 2015, he switched to the Professional Darts Corporation (PDC) and secured a two-year Tour Card on the very first day of the Qualifying School. He showcased his talent by defeating record world champion Phil Taylor at a UK Open Qualifier and qualifying for the UK Open, where he was eliminated in the second round. That same year, he achieved his first 9-darter at a Players Championship event.

De Zwaan also qualified for the European Darts Championship and the 2016 PDC World Championship, where he was eliminated in the first round of both tournaments. Despite a slump in performance that led to the loss of his Tour Card at the end of 2022, de Zwaan regained it in early 2023 with a victory at Q-School. His career in PDC youth world championships also showed some success, including reaching the semifinals in 2020.

In the image: Jeffrey de Zwaan during the semi-finals of the BetVictor World Matchplay Darts at the Winter Gardens, Blackpool, England, 2018

BENGI.NL
DRAAIJER TURBO
unicorn

DIRK VAN DUIJVENBODE

Dirk van Duijvenbode, known as "Aubergenius," has carried an eggplant as his trademark during appearances since the 2020 Darts World Championship and works on an eggplant farm alongside his darts career. Despite injuries in 2023, including one during a walk-on, he won three tournaments on the PDC Pro Tour and reached two finals on the European Darts Tour. In 2022, he continued his streak of success by claiming two more PDC titles, reaching the semifinals of the World Cup of Darts, and appearing in the final of the World Series of Darts Finals. In 2021, he secured his first PDC title at Players Championship 11 and qualified for the World Matchplay. In 2020, he reached the final of the World Grand Prix and made his debut at the European Darts Championship, advancing to the quarterfinals. Despite losing his tour card in 2018 and 2020, he fought his way back and achieved remarkable success. His international career began in 2010 at the Polish Open, and in 2014, he reached the semifinals of the PDC World Youth Championship. In August 2023, he became the father of a son.

In the image: Dirk van Duijvenbode at the Happy Bet European Darts Grand Prix in Sindelfingen, 2017

BENGI.NL
MARINE ENGINE REPAIR
Happy Bet

LUKE HUMPHRIES

His greatest success came in 2024 when he won the PDC World Championship, becoming World Champion for the first time. This victory catapulted him to the top of the world rankings. 2023 was also an outstanding year for Luke Humphries, as he claimed his first major title at the World Grand Prix and shortly after triumphed at the Grand Slam of Darts. These achievements led to further major titles, including the Players Championship Finals.

In 2022, Humphries established himself as a leading player on the European Tour, winning multiple tournaments and holding the top position in the European Tour Order of Merit. Despite some setbacks at major tournaments like the World Matchplay and the World Grand Prix, he consistently delivered strong performances.

His early successes on the PDC Development Tour in 2017 paved the way for his entry into the PDC Pro Tour. Humphries made a name for himself when he defeated reigning World Champion Rob Cross at the World Championship in 2019, although he was eliminated in the quarterfinals. That same year, he won the PDC World Youth Championship. In 2020 and 2021, he reached further significant milestones, including his first major final at the UK Open in 2021, where he defeated Michael van Gerwen before losing to James Wade.

Luke Humphries, born on February 11, 1995, in Newbury, is an English darts player who has been playing professionally since 2017 and currently leads the PDC world rankings.

In the image: Luke Humphries at the William Hill World Darts Championship at Alexandra Palace, 2018

malone

RYAN SEARLE

In 2023, Ryan Searle hit a nine-darter at the Grand Slam of Darts and reached the knockout stage but lost to eventual tournament winner Luke Humphries. At the 2024 World Championship, he was eliminated in the third round. That same year, he claimed his fifth title at the Players Championships.

In 2021, Searle made his debut at the World Matchplay and reached the quarterfinals of the World Grand Prix. He played his first major final at the 2021 Players Championship Finals, narrowly losing to Peter Wright. At the 2022 World Championship, he once again reached the last 16.

In 2020, Searle secured his first PDC title by defeating Michael van Gerwen in the final of the third Players Championship event. He also qualified for the World Grand Prix for the first time but was eliminated in the first round. At the 2021 World Championship, he again reached the last 16.

In 2018, he qualified for the Grand Slam of Darts but lost all his group stage matches. At that year's Players Championship Finals, he reached the second round and made a surprising run to the last 16 in his debut PDC World Championship.

In 2017, Searle qualified for the UK Open for the first time and reached the last 32, where he lost to Rob Cross. That same year, he also competed in the Players Championship Finals but was eliminated in the first round.

Ryan Searle, known by the nickname "Heavy Metal," first gained attention in 2013 when he reached the last 16 of the BDO World Masters after defeating Richie George in a controversial match.

In the image: Ryan Searle during his match against William O'Connor at the William Hill World Darts Championship at Alexandra Palace, London, 2018

UK VAPOUR
BRANDS

JOSÉ OLIVEIRA DE SOUSA

His greatest career achievement was winning the Grand Slam of Darts 2020, where he became the first Portuguese player to win a PDC major tournament. In the same year, he reached the third round of the PDC World Darts Championship for the first time. In 2021, he received a wildcard for the Premier League Darts, where he broke several records, including the most 180s in a single match.

José Augusto Oliveira de Sousa, born on February 25, 1974, in Azambuja, Portugal, is a darts player known by the nickname "The Special One." This name, a nod to football coach José Mourinho, also reflects de Sousa's unconventional playing style and occasional miscalculations. Active in the darts scene since 1993, he has dominated the Portuguese darts landscape ever since. He made his debut at a major tournament at the WDF World Cup 2012 and participated in the PDC World Darts Championship for the first time that same year, though he was eliminated early.

In 2019, de Sousa secured a tour card through Q-School and soon reached the final of a Players Championship, which he lost. He made history by becoming the first Portuguese player to win a Players Championship and shortly after claimed another title. In 2020, he continued his streak of success, winning the European Darts Grand Prix and throwing a nine-darter at the European Darts Championship.

Despite a challenging year in 2022, where he exited early in several tournaments, de Sousa continued to deliver impressive performances, including a Pro Tour final in April 2023. However, the year 2023 was overall disappointing for him, as his performances declined, causing him to fall significantly in the PDC Order of Merit and lose automatic qualification for major tournaments.

In the image: José Oliveira de Sousa at the NEO.bet German Dart Grand Prix in Munich, 2024

CONDOR
TRINIDAD

KEVIN PAINTER

Kevin Painter made headlines at the PDC World Darts Championship 2003 when he advanced to the semifinals. However, his most impressive performance came in 2004 when he reached the final and nearly defeated Phil Taylor. In 2011, he won his first and only major title at the Players Championship Finals. Born on July 12, 1967, in Billericay, Essex, Painter began his professional career in 1992 with the British Darts Organisation (BDO), reaching the semifinals of the Antwerp Open. His first final came at the Denmark Open, where he lost to Rod Harrington. In 1995, he claimed his first major tournament victory at the England Open and later that year won both the British Open and the British Matchplay.

In 1999, Painter switched to the Professional Darts Corporation (PDC) and reached the quarterfinals of the BDO World Darts Championship in 2000. He secured his first PDC title in 2002 at the Bob Anderson Classic. Painter solidified his position among the world's elite, reaching several semifinals at major tournaments. Despite further appearances in the last 16 at the PDC World Darts Championship, he was unable to replicate his 2011 success.

Following a decline in performance, Painter lost his Tour Card in 2019 and was unable to regain it in subsequent years. In 2021, he announced the end of his darts career but made a surprising return in 2024, appearing on the registration list for Q-School.

In the image: Kevin Painter 2024 at the World Senior Darts Championship in the Circus Tavern, Purfleet, United Kingdom

Metal Detecting
LYNETT
COMMERCIAL

Final Word

Over the years, the sport of darts has produced some of the most remarkable athletes, whose stories and achievements come to life in "The Heroes of Dart Sports: The greatest players of all time." From Phil Taylor, whose unparalleled career crowned him the king of darts, to rising talents like Gerwyn Price and Michael van Gerwen, who dominate stages around the globe, this captivating sports history spans generations. The journey through time reveals how the sport has evolved and how each player has left their own unique mark on the world of darts. The tales of triumph and determination, dramatic matches, and breathtaking throws stand as a testament to the depth and passion that darts has to offer. As the book concludes, the world of darts remains dynamic and ever-changing. New talents step onto the stage, ready to craft their own stories and perhaps one day become legends themselves. The sport, rich in history and full of promise, continues to deliver excitement and inspiration for generations of fans and players worldwide.

Impressum

For questions and suggestions: FlipFlopVerlag@gmail.com

© 2025 by FlipFlop
Oliver Kuhn
Habsburgerstrasse 8
80801 Munich

Printed in the EU

ISBN 978-3-7591-6447-6

Bildnachweise

IMAGO / IPON; IMAGO / Contrast; IMAGO / spfimages; IMAGO / Action Plus; IMAGO / Allstar; IMAGO / Future Image; IMAGO / Action Plus; IMAGO / Manngold; IMAGO / Future Image; IMAGO / Sportfoto Rudel; IMAGO / Colorsport; IMAGO / Future Image; IMAGO / Allstar; IMAGO / Allstar; IMAGO / Colorsport; IMAGO / Action Plus; IMAGO / Future Image; IMAGO / Pro Sports Images; IMAGO / Eibner; IMAGO / Pro Sports Images; IMAGO / Pressefoto Baumann; IMAGO / Avalon.red; IMAGO / Future Image; IMAGO / Action Plus; IMAGO / Panama Pictures; IMAGO / Pro Sports Images; IMAGO / PA Images; IMAGO / Action Plus; IMAGO / PA Images; IMAGO / Eibner; IMAGO / Jan Huebner; IMAGO / Pressefoto Baumann; IMAGO / Jan Huebner; IMAGO / Michael Cullen; IMAGO / Action Plus; IMAGO / Pressefoto Baumann; IMAGO / PA Images; IMAGO / PA Images; IMAGO / Harald Deubert; IMAGO/Pro Sports Images;

Printed in Dunstable, United Kingdom

75245550R00049